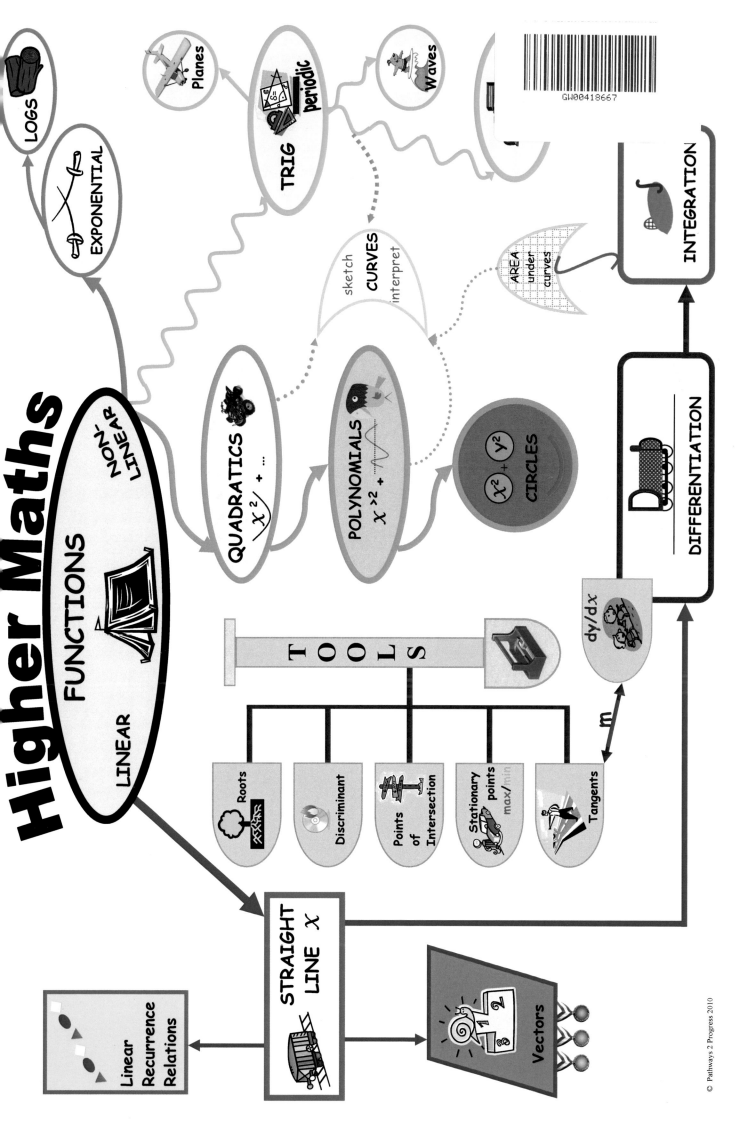

Higher Maths

LOGS

EXPONENTIAL

Planes

TRIG *periodic*

Waves

INTEGRATION

FUNCTIONS

NON-LINEAR

LINEAR

QUADRATICS $x^2 + \ldots$

POLYNOMIALS $x^{>2} + \ldots$

CIRCLES $x^2 + y^2$

sketch **CURVES** interpret

AREA under curves

DIFFERENTIATION

dy/dx

m

T O O L S

Roots

Discriminant

Points of Intersection

Stationary points *max/min*

Tangents

STRAIGHT LINE x

Linear Recurrence Relations

Vectors

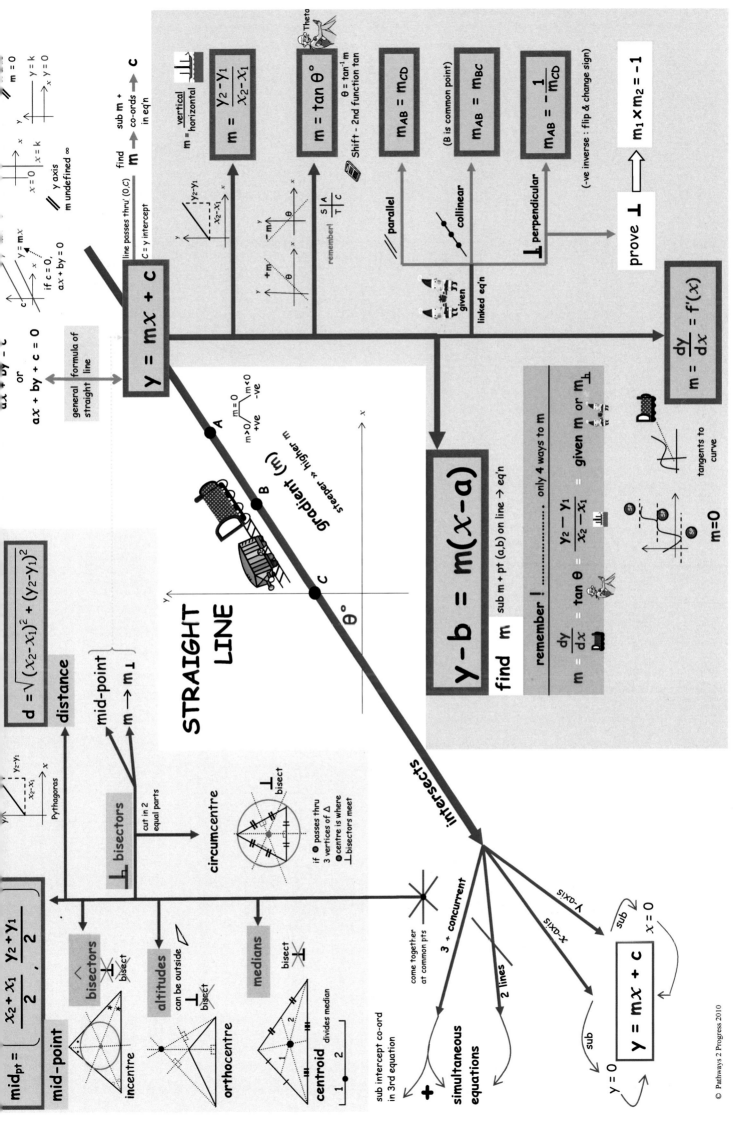

STRAIGHT LINE

$$y = mx + c$$

$$y - b = m(x - a)$$

$$m = \dfrac{dy}{dx} = f'(x)$$

$$d = \sqrt{(x_2 - x_1)^2 + (y_2 - y_1)^2}$$ distance

mid-point

$$mid_{pt} = \left(\dfrac{x_2 + x_1}{2} , \dfrac{y_2 + y_1}{2} \right)$$

mid-point

$m \rightarrow m_\perp$

gradient (m) steeper → higher

$m > 0$ +ve $m < 0$ -ve $m = 0$

θ°

$$m = \dfrac{vertical}{horizontal}$$

$$m = \dfrac{y_2 - y_1}{x_2 - x_1}$$

$$m = \tan θ°$$

θ = tan⁻¹ m

Shift - 2nd function tan

$$m_{AB} = m_{CD}$$ parallel

$$m_{AB} = m_{BC}$$ collinear (B is common point)

$$m_{AB} = -\dfrac{1}{m_{CD}}$$ perpendicular

(-ve inverse : flip & change sign)

$$m_1 \times m_2 = -1$$ prove ⊥

line passes thru (0,c)
c = y intercept

find **m**

sub m + co-ords in eq'n

$m = 0$ $y = k$ $x = 0$ $y = 0$

$x = 0$ y axis
m undefined ∞ $x = k$

$y = mx$ if $c = 0$, $ax + by = 0$

general straight line — formula of straight line

$ax + by = c$ or $ax + by + c = 0$

S | A
T | C
remember!

find **m** sub m + pt (a,b) on line → eq'n

remember ! .... only 4 ways to m

$$m = \dfrac{dy}{dx} = \tan θ = \dfrac{y_2 - y_1}{x_2 - x_1} = given\ m\ or\ m_\perp$$

tangents to curve

SP   SP   SP

$m = 0$

intersects

sub intercept co-ord in 3rd equation

3 + concurrent come together at common pts

simultaneous equations 2 lines

x-axis   y-axis

$y = mx + c$

sub $x = 0$

sub $y = 0$

bisectors

cut in 2 equal parts

⊥ bisectors

circumcentre

if ● passes thru 3 vertices of △
● centre is where ⊥ bisectors meet

bisect

bisectors bisect

incentre

altitudes can be outside ⊥ bisect

orthocentre

medians bisect

centroid divides median 1 | 2

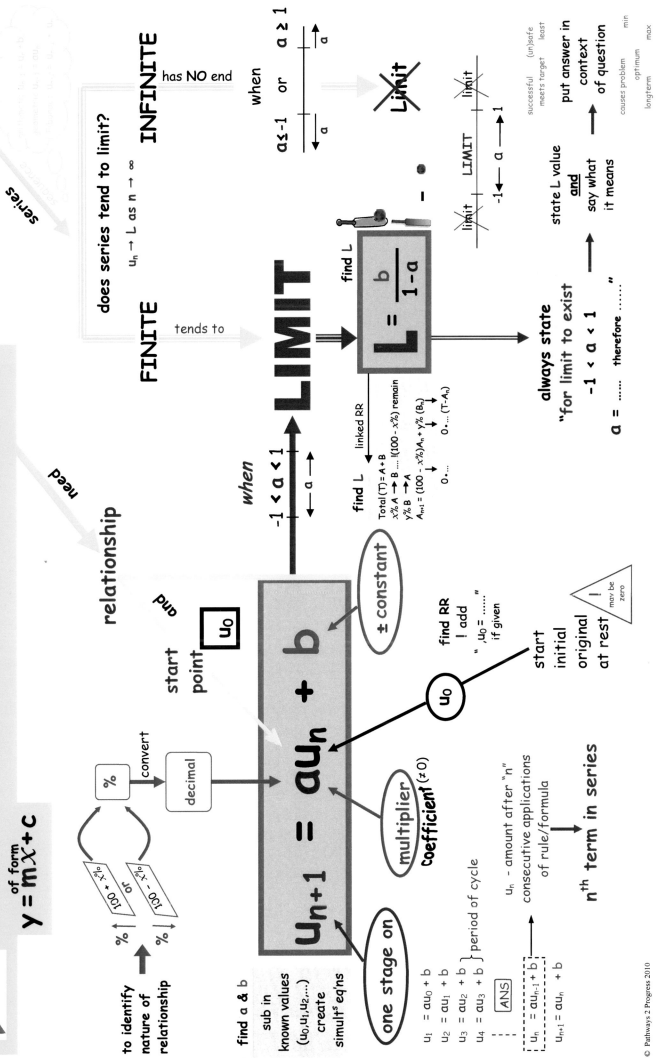

LINEAR RECURRENCE RELATIONS

of form
$y = mx + c$

terms are predictable

series

sequence

does series tend to limit?
$u_n \to L$ as $n \to \infty$

INFINITE
has NO end

when

$a \leq -1$ or $a \geq 1$

~~Limit~~

~~limit~~ ~~limit~~

LIMIT

$-1 \leftarrow a \rightarrow 1$

successful (un)safe
meets target least
put answer in context of question

causes problem min
optimum
longterm max

state L value **and** say what it means

FINITE
tends to

LIMIT

find L

$$L = \frac{b}{1-a}$$

always state
"for limit to exist
$-1 < a < 1$
$a = \ldots$ therefore ...."

when
$-1 < a < 1$
$a \rightarrow$

linked RR

find L
Total (T) = A + B
$x\% A \to B \ldots !(100 - x\%)$ remain
$y\% B \to A$
$A_{n+1} = (100 - x\%)A_n + y\% (B_n)$
$0 \ldots (T-A_n)$
$0 \ldots$

need

relationship

start point
u_0

and

$\pm$ constant

find RR
! add
" $, u_0 = \ldots$ "
if given

u_0

start
initial
original
at rest

!
may be zero

to identify nature of relationship

% convert decimal

$100 + x\%$ or $100 - x\%$
% %

$$u_{n+1} = au_n + b$$

multiplier
coefficient $(\neq 0)$

one stage on

u_n – amount after "n" consecutive applications of rule/formula

n^{th} **term in series**

find a & b
sub in known values
$(u_0, u_1, u_2, \ldots)$
create simult^s eq'ns

$u_1 = au_0 + b$
$u_2 = au_1 + b$
$u_3 = au_2 + b$
$u_4 = au_3 + b$ } period of cycle

ANS

$u_n = au_{n-1} + b$
$u_{n+1} = au_n + b$

© Pathways 2 Progress 2010

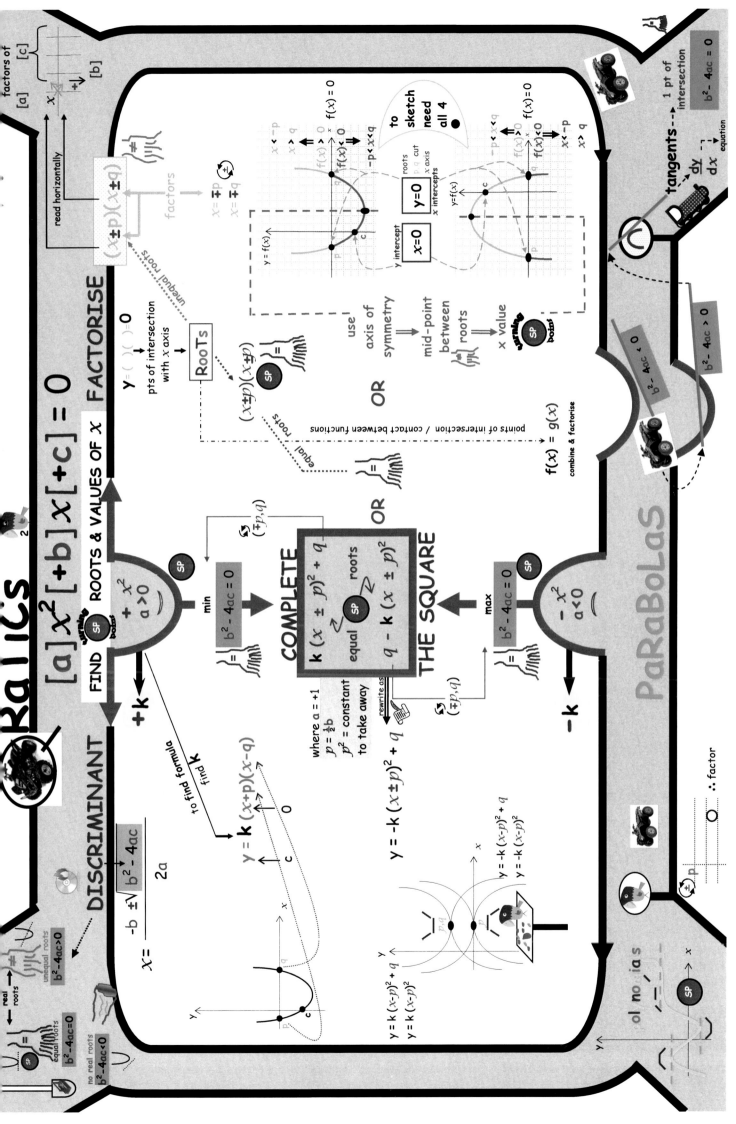

TOOLS

quadratics
parabola
polynomials
circles

prove tangent

set $f(x) = g(x)$
$y_1 = y_2$

> 2 points of intersection

no point of intersection

1 point of intersection

>1 point of intersection

polynomial

$x \pm h) \rightarrow$ $\mp h$ 2 3 4 5
change sign!

$\dfrac{0}{\quad}$ $f(x) = 0$ ▸▸ factor

2

find contact pts
→ factorise
• common factor
• diff 2 □ 's
• ( )( )

roots
values at point
of intersection
or contact

$x = \dfrac{-b \pm \sqrt{b^2 - 4ac}}{2a}$

$ax^2 + bx + c = 0$

discriminant

$b^2 - 4ac$

prove tangent   use

sub / eq'n into ● eq'n

find contact point(s) use

factorise ( )( )

no real roots
(no values for x)

equal (real) roots
$(x \pm p)^2$

(unequal) **real** roots
$(x \pm p)(x \pm q)$

$b^2 - 4ac < 0$

$b^2 - 4ac = 0$

$b^2 - 4ac > 0$

$m_\perp$

$y_1 = y_2$

SP
highest → greatest → most
optimum → max → fastest
quickest
min
smallest → least
Point of inflection
lowest
continues ↕
slowest → cheapest

differentiate
then sub in "known" x
value to get value of **m**

SP

$m^{(-ve)}$ nature table $m^{(+ve)}$

$\dfrac{dy}{dx} < 0$ $\dfrac{dy}{dx} > 0$

$m = \dfrac{dy}{dx} = 0$ SP !

• (a,b)

$$y - b = m(x - a)$$

remember ! ......
only **4** ways
to **m**

$m_\perp$

or

$y = mx + c$

rearrange
given eq'n

$= \dfrac{y_2 - y_1}{x_2 - x_1}$

$= \tan \theta°$

$= \dfrac{dy}{dx}$ $f'(x)$

find equation of tangent / straight line

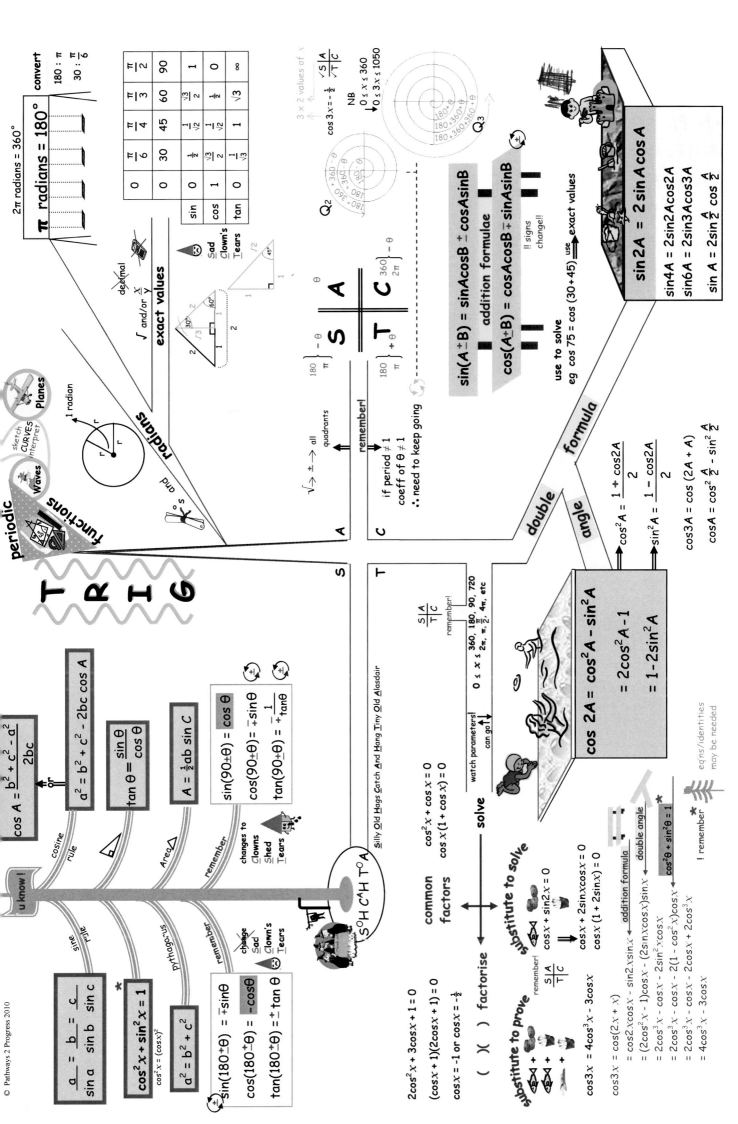

© Pathways 2 Progress 2010

periodic functions   Waves   Planes   sketch CURVES interpret

T R I G

2π radians = 360°

convert — 180 : π ; 30 : π/6

π radians = 180°

	0	$\frac{\pi}{6}$	$\frac{\pi}{4}$	$\frac{\pi}{3}$	$\frac{\pi}{2}$
	0	30	45	60	90
sin	0	$\frac{1}{2}$	$\frac{1}{\sqrt2}$	$\frac{\sqrt3}{2}$	1
cos	1	$\frac{\sqrt3}{2}$	$\frac{1}{\sqrt2}$	$\frac{1}{2}$	0
tan	0	$\frac{1}{\sqrt3}$	1	$\sqrt3$	∞

exact values — ~~decimal~~ ; $\sqrt{\ }$ and/or $\frac{x}{y}$

Sad / Clown's / Tears

radians — 1 radian ; and

u know!

cosine rule
$$\cos A = \frac{b^2 + c^2 - a^2}{2bc}\quad\text{or}\quad a^2 = b^2 + c^2 - 2bc\cos A$$

sine rule
$$\frac{a}{\sin a} = \frac{b}{\sin b} = \frac{c}{\sin c}$$

pythagoras
$$\cos^2 x + \sin^2 x = 1$$
$$\cos^2 x = (\cos x)^2$$
$$a^2 = b^2 + c^2$$

Area △
$$A = \tfrac{1}{2}ab\sin C$$

$$\tan\theta = \frac{\sin\theta}{\cos\theta}$$

remember
$$\sin(90\pm\theta) = \cos\theta$$
$$\cos(90\pm\theta) = \mp\sin\theta$$
$$\tan(90\pm\theta) = \mp\frac{1}{\tan\theta}$$
changes to Clowns Shed Tears

$$\sin(180\mp\theta) = \pm\sin\theta$$
$$\cos(180\mp\theta) = -\cos\theta$$
$$\tan(180\mp\theta) = \mp\tan\theta$$
change Sad Clown's Tears

$S^OH\ C^AH\ T^O A$

Silly Old Hags Catch And Hang Tiny Old Alasdair

$2\cos^2 x + 3\cos x + 1 = 0$
$(\cos x + 1)(2\cos x + 1) = 0$
$\cos x = -1$ or $\cos x = -\tfrac{1}{2}$

solve
$\cos^2 x + \cos x = 0$
$\cos x(1 + \cos x) = 0$

common factors

$(\ )(\ )$ **factorise**

substitute to prove   remember! $\frac{S|A}{T|C}$

substitute to solve
$\cos x + \sin 2x = 0$
$\cos x + 2\sin x\cos x = 0$
$\cos x(1 + 2\sin x) = 0$

$\cos 3x = 4\cos^3 x - 3\cos x$
$\cos 3x = \cos(2x + x)$
$= \cos 2x\cos x - \sin 2x \times \sin x$ — addition formula
$= (2\cos^2 x - 1)\cos x - (2\sin x\cos x)\sin x$
$= 2\cos^3 x - \cos x - 2\sin^2 x\times\cos x$
$= 2\cos^3 x - \cos x - 2(1 - \cos^2 x)\cos x$
$= 2\cos^3 x - \cos x - 2\cos x + 2\cos^3 x$
$= 4\cos^3 x - 3\cos x$

double angle
$\cos^2\theta + \sin^2\theta = 1$
! remember

watch parameters! can go!
$0 \le x \le 360,\ 180,\ 90,\ 720,\ 2\pi,\ \pi,\ \tfrac{\pi}{2},\ 4\pi,\ \text{etc}$
remember! $\frac{S|A}{T|C}$

3×2 values of x
$\cos 3x = -\tfrac{1}{2}$
NB $0 \le x \le 360$, $0 \le 3x \le 1050$

$\frac{A\ |\ S}{T\ |\ C}$ $\frac{180}{\pi}\Big\}-\theta$ $\frac{360}{2\pi}\Big\}-\theta$ $\frac{180}{\pi}\Big\}+\theta$

remember! if period ≠ 1, coeff of θ ≠ 1 ∴ need to keep going

$\sqrt{\ } \rightarrow \pm \rightarrow$ all quadrants

addition formulae
$$\sin(A\pm B) = \sin A\cos B \pm \cos A\sin B$$
$$\cos(A\mp B) = \cos A\cos B \pm \sin A\sin B$$
!! signs change!!

use to solve eg $\cos 75 = \cos(30+45) \xrightarrow{use}$ exact values

double angle formula
$$\cos 2A = \cos^2 A - \sin^2 A = 2\cos^2 A - 1 = 1 - 2\sin^2 A$$
$$\sin 2A = 2\sin A\cos A$$
$$\sin 4A = 2\sin 2A\cos 2A$$
$$\sin 6A = 2\sin 3A\cos 3A$$
$$\sin A = 2\sin\tfrac{A}{2}\cos\tfrac{A}{2}$$

$$\cos^2 A = \frac{1 + \cos 2A}{2}$$
$$\sin^2 A = \frac{1 - \cos 2A}{2}$$
$$\cos 3A = \cos(2A + A)$$
$$\cos A = \cos^2\tfrac{A}{2} - \sin^2\tfrac{A}{2}$$

eq'ns/identities may be needed

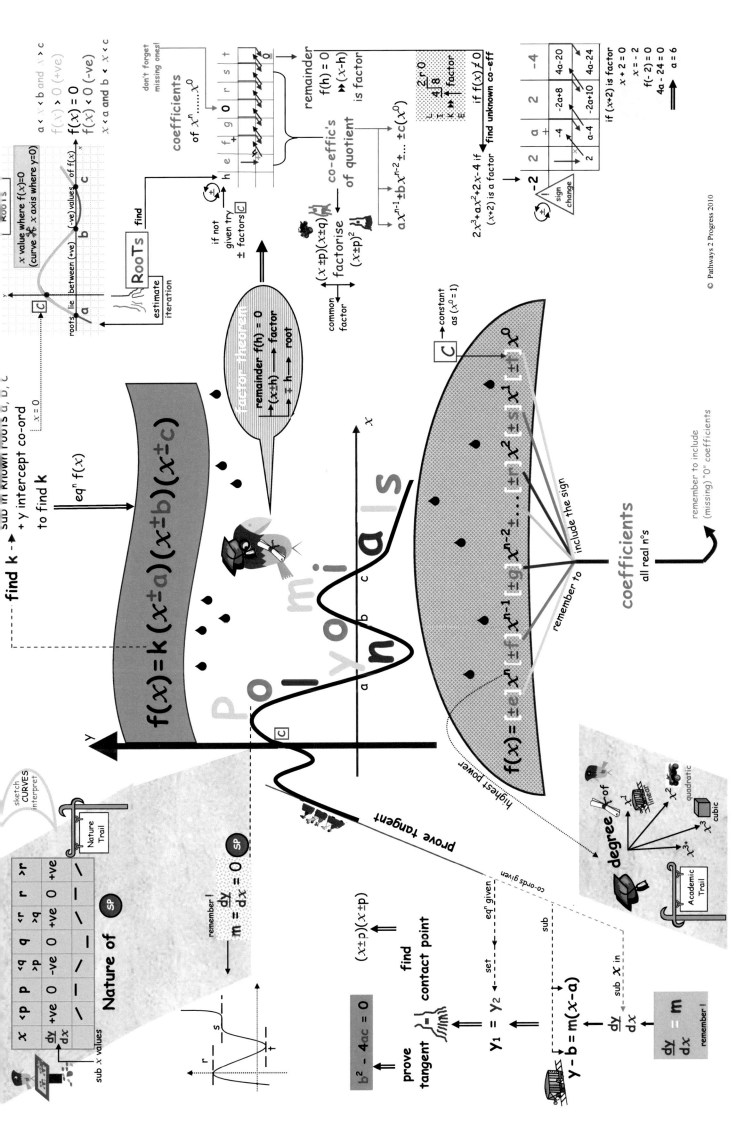

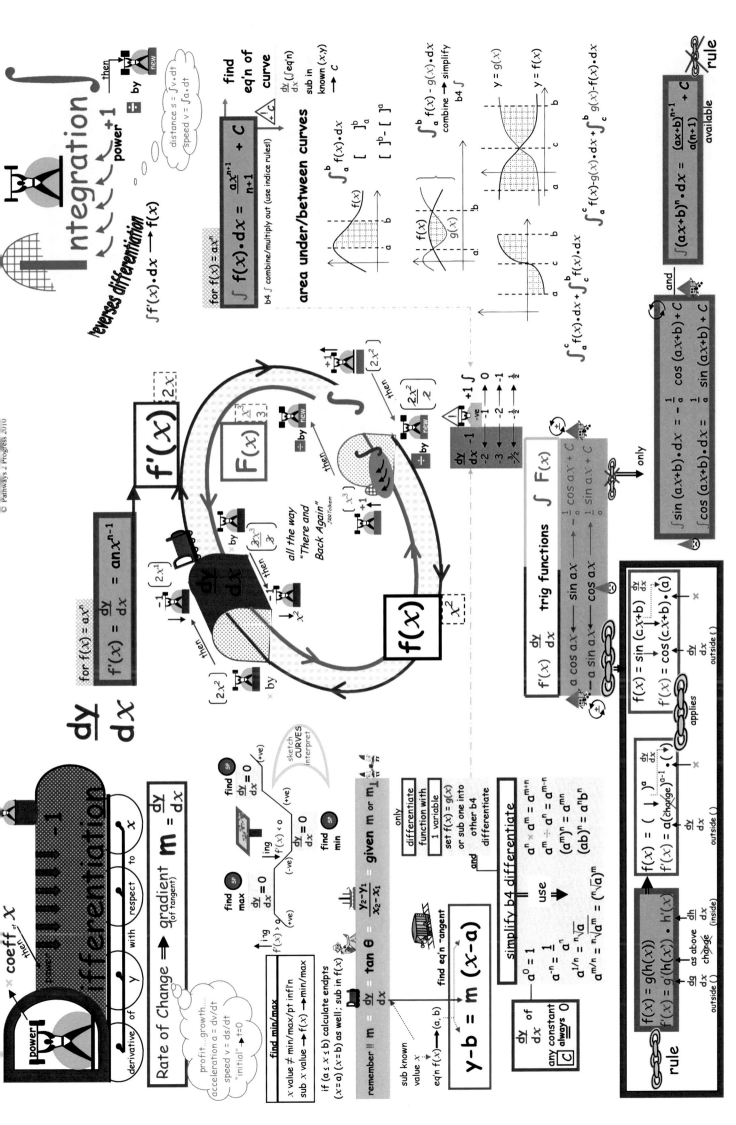

© Pathways 2 Progress 2010

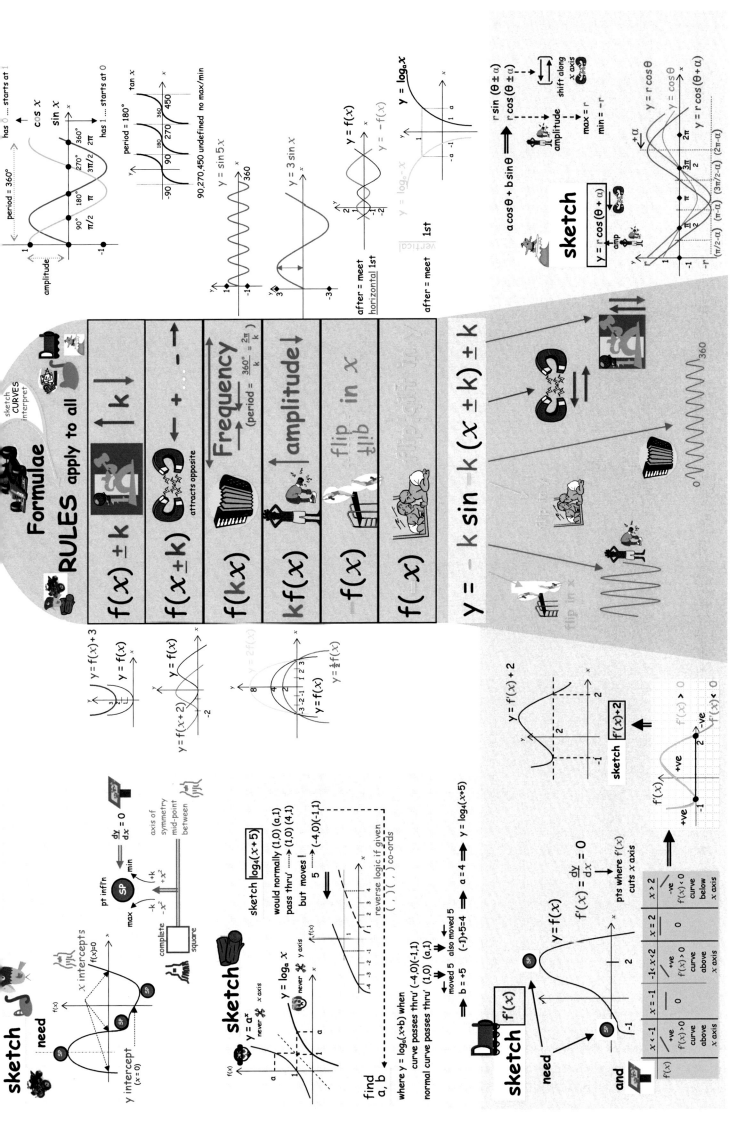

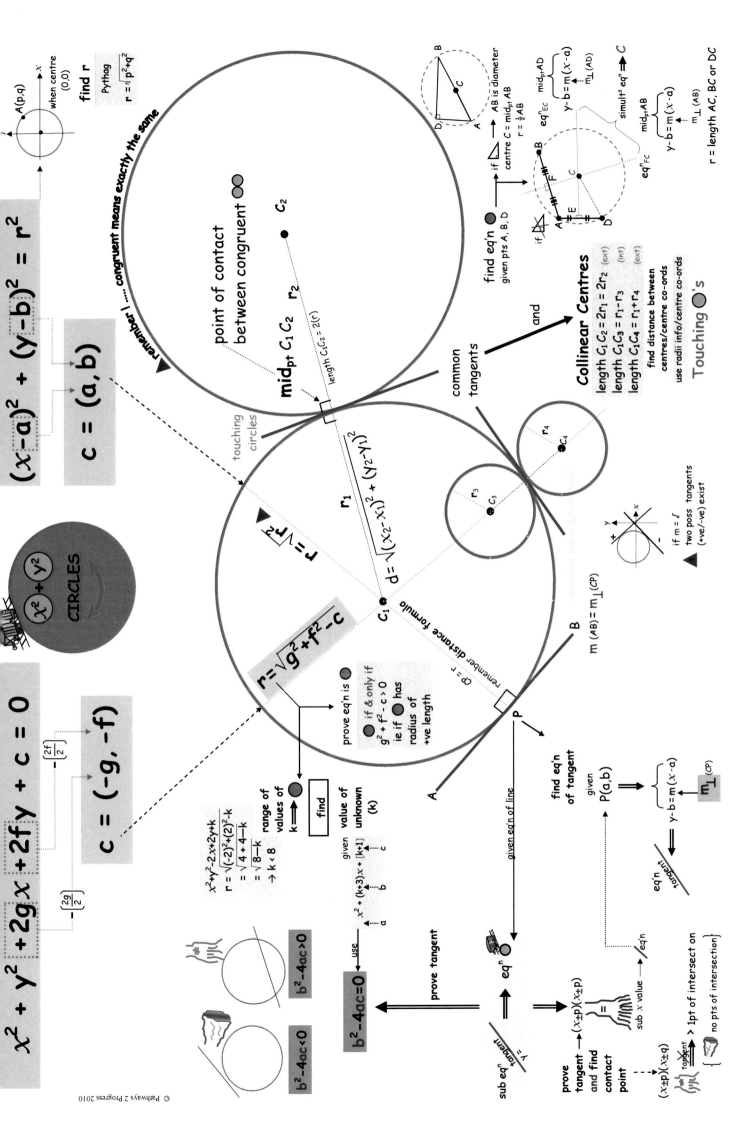

$x^2 + y^2 + 2gx + 2fy + c = 0$

$c = (-g, -f)$

$-\frac{2g}{2}$ $-\frac{2f}{2}$

CIRCLES
$x^2 + y^2$

when centre (0,0)

find r
Pythag $r = \sqrt{p^2 + q^2}$

A(p,q)

$(x-a)^2 + (y-b)^2 = r^2$

$c = (a, b)$

remember | ... congruent means exactly the same

point of contact between congruent

C_2

$mid_{pt}\ C_1 C_2$ r_2

length $C_1 C_2 = 2(r)$

touching circles

r_1

$d = \sqrt{(x_2-x_1)^2 + (y_2-y_1)^2}$

remember distance formula

C_1

$r = \sqrt{r^2}$

$r = \sqrt{g^2 + f^2 - c}$

prove eq'n is
● if & only if $g^2 + f^2 - c > 0$
ie if ● has radius of +ve length

range of values of k < 8

$x^2 + y^2 - 2x + 2y + k$
$r = \sqrt{(-2)^2 + (2)^2 - k}$
$= \sqrt{4 + 4 - k}$
$= \sqrt{8 - k}$
→ k < 8

find
value of unknown (k)

given
$x^2 + (k+3)x + [k+1]$
  a   b   c

use $b^2 - 4ac = 0$

$b^2 - 4ac > 0$
$b^2 - 4ac < 0$

prove tangent

sub eq'n
$y = $

prove tangent and find contact point
$(x \pm p)(x \pm q)$

tangent
x_{int} > 1pt of intersect on
{ no pts of intersection }

sub x value → eq'n
$= (x \pm p)(x \pm p)$

given eq'n of line

$CP = r$

$m (AB) = m_\perp (CP)$

A B P

find eq'n of tangent
given P(a,b)
$\Rightarrow$ y - b = m(x - a)
$m_\perp (CP)$

eq'n tangent

if m = ∫ two poss tangents (+ve/-ve) exist

common tangents and

r_3 C_3 r_4 C_4

Collinear Centres
length $C_1 C_2 = 2r_1 = 2r_2$ (ext)
length $C_1 C_3 = r_1 - r_3$ (int)
length $C_1 C_4 = r_1 + r_4$ (ext)

find distance between centres/centre co-ords
use radii info/centre co-ords

Touching ●'s

if ↑ AB is diameter
centre $C = mid_{pt}\ AB$
$r = \frac{1}{2}AB$

find eq'n
given pts A, B, D

B C D A

eq^n_{EC} $mid_{pt} AD$
y - b = m(x - a)
$m_\perp (AD)$

eq^n_{FC} $mid_{pt} AB$
y - b = m(x - a)
$m_\perp (AB)$

simult^s eq^n ⟹ C

r = length AC, BC or DC

© Pathways 2 Progress 2010

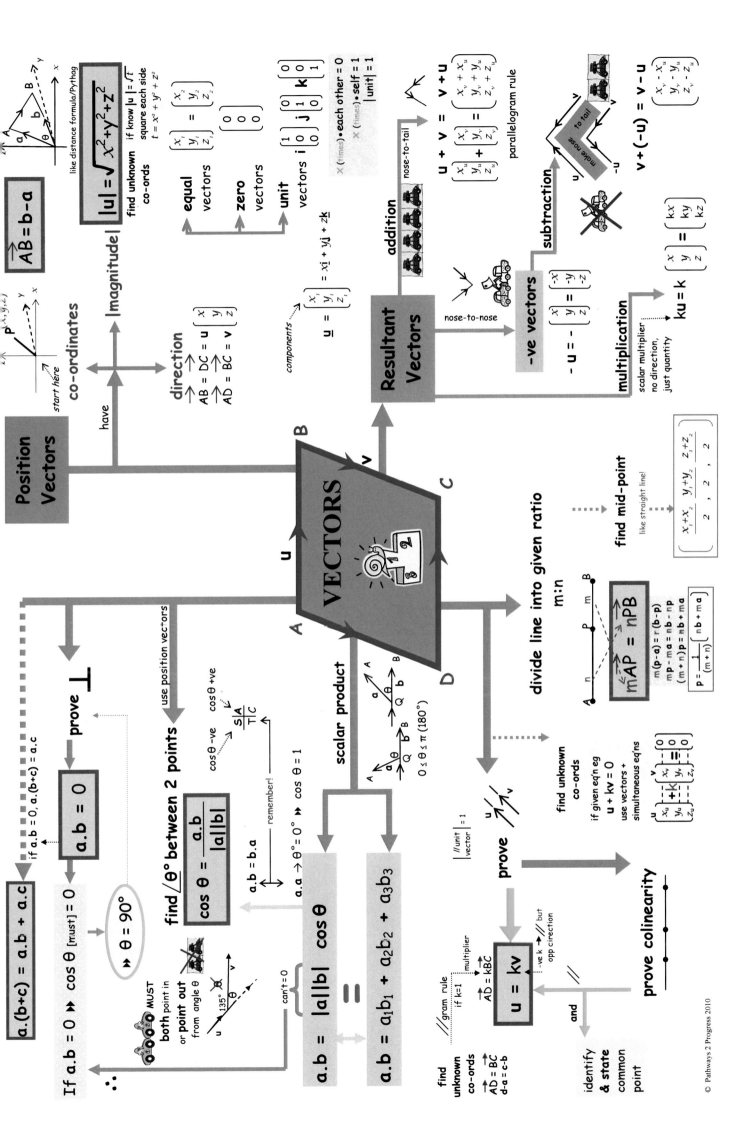

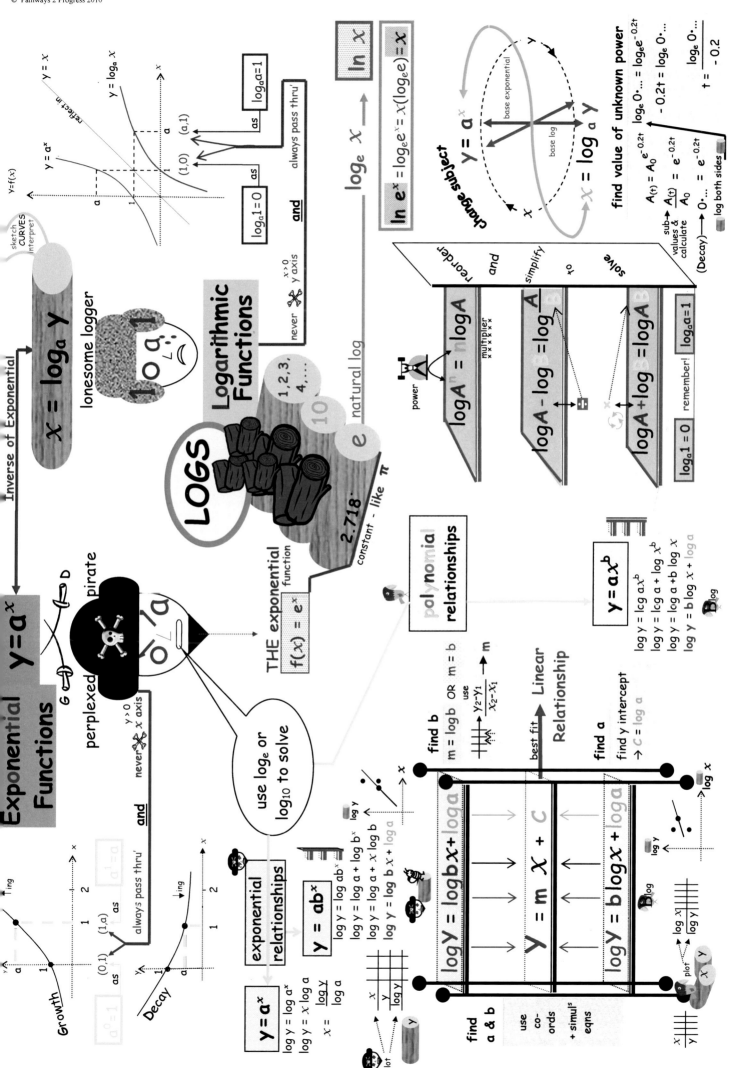

© Pathways 2 Progress 2010

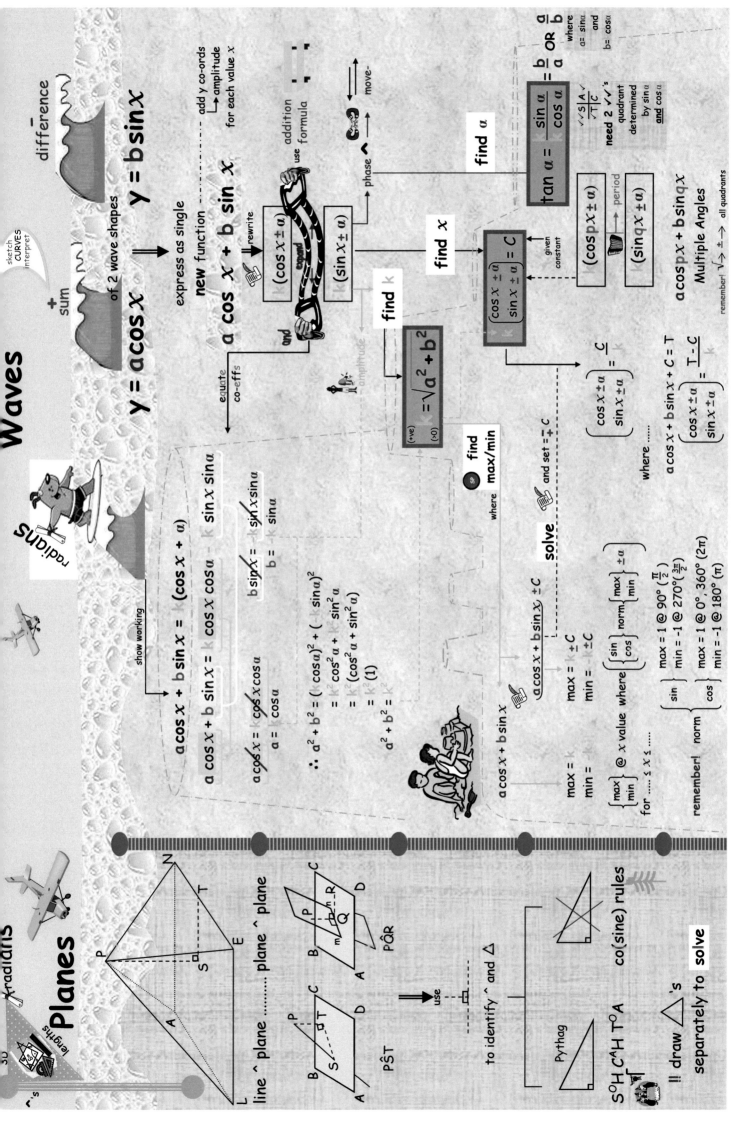

Waves

difference −

sum +

of 2 wave shapes

$y = a\cos x$
$y = b\sin x$

sketch CURVES interpret

add y co-ords → amplitude for each value x

express as single **new function**
$a\cos x + b\sin x$

rewrite

use addition formula

$k(\cos x \pm \alpha)$

and

$k(\sin x \pm \alpha)$

phase ^ move-

find α

$\tan \alpha = \dfrac{\sin \alpha}{\cos \alpha} = \dfrac{b}{a}$ OR $\dfrac{a}{b}$

where
$a = \sin\alpha$ and
$b = \cos\alpha$

$\dfrac{\sqrt{S}\,|\,A\sqrt{}}{\sqrt{}\,T\,|\,C}$

need 2 √√'s quadrant determined by $\sin\alpha$ **and** $\cos\alpha$

find x

$\begin{pmatrix}\cos x \pm \alpha\\ \sin x \pm \alpha\end{pmatrix} = C$

given constant

$k(\cos px \pm \alpha)$
$k(\sin qx \pm \alpha)$
period

$a\cos px + b\sin qx$
Multiple Angles
remember! $\sqrt{} \to \pm \leftrightarrow$ all quadrants

find k

$k = \sqrt{a^2 + b^2}$
(+ve) (>0)

SP find max/min
where ......

and set $= \pm c$

solve
$a\cos x + b\sin x \pm C$

equate co-effs

amplitude

show working

$a\cos x + b\sin x = k(\cos x + \alpha)$

$a\cos x + b\sin x = k\cos x \cos\alpha - k\sin x \sin\alpha$

$b\sin x = -k\sin x \sin\alpha$
$b = -k\sin\alpha$

$a\cos x = k\cos x \cos\alpha$
$a = k\cos\alpha$

$\therefore a^2 + b^2 = (k\cos\alpha)^2 + (-k\sin\alpha)^2$
$= k^2\cos^2\alpha + k^2\sin^2\alpha$
$= k^2(\cos^2\alpha + \sin^2\alpha)$
$= k^2(1)$
$a^2 + b^2 = k^2$

$a\cos x + b\sin x \pm C$
max $= k \pm C$
min $= -k \pm C$

$\begin{pmatrix}\cos x \pm \alpha\\ \sin x \pm \alpha\end{pmatrix} = \dfrac{C}{k}$

where ......

$a\cos x + b\sin x + C = T$
$\begin{pmatrix}\cos x \pm \alpha\\ \sin x \pm \alpha\end{pmatrix} = \dfrac{T-C}{k}$

max $= k$
min $= -k$
for ..... $\leq x \leq$ ......

$\begin{bmatrix}max\\min\end{bmatrix}$ @ x value where $\begin{bmatrix}\sin\\\cos\end{bmatrix}$ norm $\begin{bmatrix}max\\min\end{bmatrix} \pm\alpha$

remember! norm $\begin{bmatrix}\sin\\\cos\end{bmatrix}$

sin: max = 1 @ 90° $\left(\frac{\pi}{2}\right)$, min = -1 @ 270° $\left(\frac{3\pi}{2}\right)$

cos: max = 1 @ 0°, 360° (2π), min = -1 @ 180° (π)

radians

Planes

3D lengths ^'s

line ^ plane ...... plane ^ plane

PŜT

PQR

to identify ^ and △

use

Pythag

S^OH C^AH T^OA

co(sine) rules

!! draw △'s separately to **solve**

radians | π = 180°

AL the Clown's

6 easy steps

to the

Exact Value Table

only need to recall 6 nos.

0 90 6 1

$\frac{1}{\sqrt{2}}$ $\frac{\sqrt{3}}{2}$

Complete the table this way every time you sit down to problem solve (check it) and you will be able to write it out easily and accurately at the start of each exam.

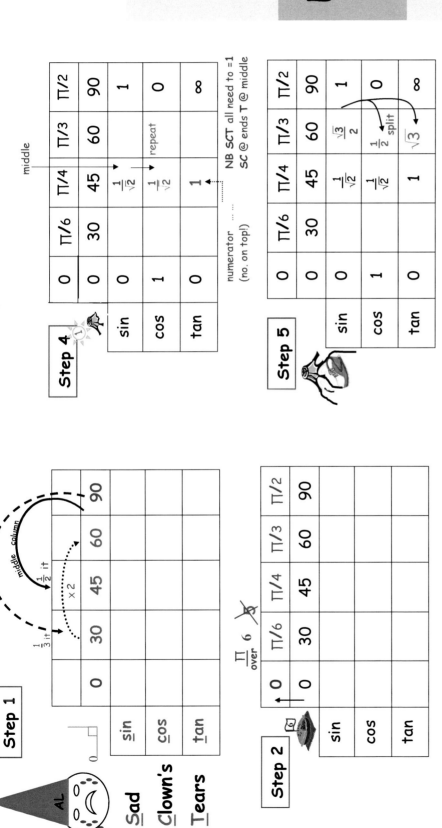

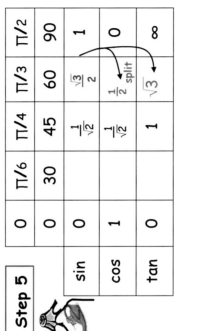

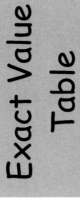

Step 1

AL — Sad / Clown's / Tears

	0	30	45	60	90
sin					
cos					
tan					

middle column · $\frac{1}{3}$ it · ×2 · $\frac{1}{2}$ it

Step 2

$\frac{\pi}{\text{over}}$ 6

	0	π/6	π/4	π/3	π/2
	0	30	45	60	90
sin	0				
cos					
tan					

Step 3

	0	π/6	π/4	π/3	π/2
	0	30	45	60	90
sin	0				1
cos	1				0
tan	0				∞ undefined

continue pattern · the empty box!

Step 4

middle

	0	π/6	π/4	π/3	π/2
	0	30	45	60	90
sin	0		$\frac{1}{\sqrt{2}}$		1
cos	0		$\frac{1}{\sqrt{2}}$	repeat	0
tan	0		1		∞

numerator (no. on top!)

NB SCT all need to =1
SC @ ends T @ middle

Step 5

	0	π/6	π/4	π/3	π/2
	0	30	45	60	90
sin	0		$\frac{1}{\sqrt{2}}$	$\frac{\sqrt{3}}{2}$	1
cos	0		$\frac{1}{\sqrt{2}}$	$\frac{1}{2}$ split	0
tan	0		1	$\sqrt{3}$	∞

Step 6

	0	π/6	π/4	π/3	π/2
	0	30	45	60	90
sin	0	$\frac{1}{2}$	$\frac{1}{\sqrt{2}}$	$\frac{\sqrt{3}}{2}$	1
cos	1	$\frac{\sqrt{3}}{2}$	$\frac{1}{\sqrt{2}}$	$\frac{1}{2}$	0
tan	0	$\frac{1}{\sqrt{3}}$	1	$\sqrt{3}$	∞

inverse

AL the Clown's Exact Value Table
STEPS a–l

AL

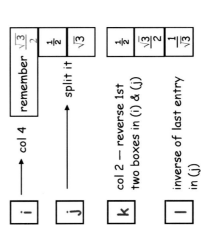

	c	0	π/6	π/4	π/3	π/2
			6	4 ✗	3	2
a		d 0	30	45	60	e 90
b Sad	sin	drop down 0	k ½	g 1/√2	i √3/2	continue pattern 1
Clown's	cos	1	√3/2	1/√2	j ½ (split)	0
Tears	tan	0	l 1/√3	h 1	√3	f ∞

NB SCT all need to =1
SC @ ends T @ middle

---

only need to remember 6 number facts

0 90 6 1 1/√2 √3/2

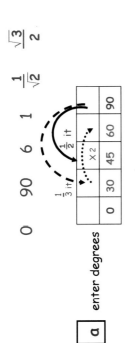

a enter degrees

b name rows — Sad Clown's Tears

c enter radians — π over 6 ✗4 3 2

d drop down col 1 and complete
| 0 |
| 1 |
| 0 |

e continue pattern
| 1 |
| 0 |
| ∞ |

f and the one you can't define

g go to middle ccl 3
remember 1/√2
repeat 1/√2
1

h take top no. — 1

---

i → col 4 — remember
| √3/2 |
| ½ |
| √3 |

j split it
| ½ |
| √3/2 |
| 1/√3 |

k col 2 — reverse 1st two boxes in (i) & (j)

l inverse of last entry in (j)

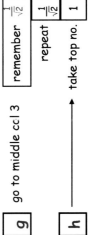